CPE Workbook

Character, Plot, & Emotion

The Three Foundational Pillars of Storytelling

Diana Stout

Michael Hauge's material used with permission.

Cover design: Sharpened Pencils Productions LLC

ISBN: 979-8-9870751-5-9

With *CPE: Character, Plot and Emotion,* Diana Stout brilliantly reveals and edifies the uniquely powerful principles of plot and character created by eight writers and consultants who are regarded as masters of storytelling for film and fiction. But the real treasure of this wonderful book is how she simplifies and combines their methods with her own expertise as a hugely accomplished novelist, teacher, and consultant. The result (along with its accompanying workbook) is an essential guide to transforming the emotional impact and commercial success of your own storytelling.

Michael Hauge, author of *Writing Screenplays That Sell, Selling Your Story in 60 Seconds, The Hero's Two Journeys* (with Christopher Vogler), and *Storytelling Made Easy* (for business leaders, speakers, and entrepreneurs)

*****

"The worksheets are easy-to-use, a real time-saver. They have helped me add depth, find holes, and redefine my stories." – Linda Bradley, author

*****

"I was shocked to see three of the five major plot points were missing... I'm a visual learner and Diana's method has shown me that plotting, which I called outlining isn't at all like the outlining we used to do in high school classes!" Diana Lloyd, author

*****

"In the past, I'd run seeing the 12 steps [of plotting]. I didn't understand them or the percentages at key points." – Linda Fletcher, writer

*****

"I've tried different methods of plotting and various beat sheet methods. Nothing worked well for me. I always felt that something was lacking... Emotion was the missing component.... These CPE worksheets gave my story a rudder." – L M English, writer

DEDICATION

For those writers who purchased *CPE,*
learning the *why* behind the
character, plotting, and emotion structural pillars,
and who wanted to create my character and plotting worksheets easily.

For those writers who didn't purchase *CPE*
and wanted to shortcut, going straight into using plotting worksheets.

May you all succeed in your trying, your writing,
and in improving your writing process.

CONTENTS

ACKNOWLEDGEMENTS

Thank you to my beta testers, Lenore, the two Lindas, and the other Diana who took my initial plotting sheets and various revisions of them, and tried them out, giving me excellent feedback in return.

And, once again, a standing ovation to the three writers—Christopher Vogler, Michael Hauge, and Allen Palmer—who by sharing their discoveries changed my plotting and storytelling abilities forever, providing me with delightful *aha moments.*

May every writer who purchases this workbook find it useful and provide you with a lifetime of *aha moments* as you plot forth your stories.

CPE Workbook

Character, Plot, & Emotion

The Three Foundational Pillars of Storytelling

Pantser – Someone who writes without a plot or a plan; it's minimal and in their head.

Plotter – Someone who creates a written plan before writing their first draft.

Plantser – Someone who both plots *and* pantsers.

CHAPTER 1 – WHY A WORKBOOK?

The short answer...

The pantser beta testers of my plotting worksheets and those who became my beta readers for the finished *CPE* book asked if I was going to provide worksheets to the readers.

They were enthused and wanted me to share what they were learning. In their excitement, they wanted you to have the same opportunities they'd had—chiefly, full-size worksheets!

The long answer...

Originally, I started writing *CPE,* the how-to resource guide, as an 8.5 x 11″ book but then abandoned that size, creating a 5.5 x 8.5″ size so that it would match the rest of the writing how-to series I was developing. The first book—*Finding Your Fire & Keeping It Hot*—was already published.

As the beta readers and I started brainstorming different solutions, the best answer was to create a separate workbook where the writer could scan or tear certain pages out of the book for duplicating or scanning.

Why *this* Workbook?

Even though I had written three romances and was in the process of selling them through traditional publishers, I didn't learn about storytelling plot structure until I began reading screenwriting books by Syd Field, Christopher Vogler, Michael Hauge, and John Truby. It would be another decade before I'd learned about Blake Snyder.

I had so many *aha moments* in that learning. Even though I was reading the books and writing screenplays, it would be that first long weekend seminar with Michael Hauge in Atlanta where I had one *aha moment* after another.

I never thought about applying screenwriting techniques to my fictional novel characters until that workshop. Once I did, my writing changed forever.

As I learned from others and began experimenting, adapting their processes, and changing them bit-by-bit so they worked for me, I discovered the magic of plotting that became *my* process. The secret was manipulating or adapting a process until it worked and eliminating anything that didn't work.

As a result, I was writing faster, was eliminating the sagging middle, and was no longer requiring plot-heavy rewrites. The holes were fixed before I started writing the first draft!

I had become more of a plotter than a pantser.

> *Pantser – Someone who writes without a plot or a plan. If they do have a plan, it's minimal and usually in their head.*
>
> *Plotter – Someone who creates a written plan—anywhere from minimal to detailed—before they begin writing their first draft.*

In the process, I discovered none of us are 100 percent one or the other. We're a combination of both. Some of us pantser more than we plot. Others plot more than they pantser. Essentially, we're *plantsers.*

How Can This Workbook Help Me?

If you struggle with a sagging middle, have flat one-dimensional characters, get stuck and aren't sure where to go next, or have lost interest in your story, this workbook can help eliminate those negatives.

If you're a pantser, yet have had issues with any of the above topics, you may want to consider how the tiniest bit of plotting could turn those negatives into positives and have you feeling energized and passionate about your story again.

Eliminating the Myths of Plotting

Plotting is nothing like high school outlining. That kind of outlining works for dissertations, proposals, nonfiction, technical, and business writing, but not for fiction.

Plotting story doesn't eliminate all surprises in the writing. For example, I'm a heavy plotter, but I'm pantsering in most every scene. I get surprised by my characters' dialogue, even in the events as they unfold.

What Story Plotting Looks Like

If you've ever written a synopsis, you were plotting. If you know the ending of your story or what happens in a few scenes, you're plotting.

If you write screenplay treatments, which is another word for synopsis, you're plotting.

Plotting doesn't require pages and pages of details. In fact, the best way to determine if plotting will work for you is to start with minimal plotting. I'll show you how to do that once we encounter the plotting worksheets later in this workbook.

The Goal of This Book

My goal for writing this supplemental companion book is to present summary information tied to the *CPE* book and worksheets that can help *your* writing process.

Your goal is to figure out which elements and ideas will help you the most right away, and incorporate them into your writing process as you plot this story or the next one.

Maybe you're struggling with a story right now, and you want to re-plot the story and upgrade your process. That's doable, too.

Just as various writing programs upgrade their writing programs, we want to upgrade our writing process from time to time, as well.

Even though I often think that I won't be upgrading my process ever again, *surprise!* Something I read or hear will have me tweaking my process. Sometimes, it's just adding a small element. Sometimes, it's streamlining my process because I've found a shortcut.

I don't know about you, but I love, love, *love* shortcuts!

That's what I was doing with every *aha moment* I experienced. Upgrading. Changing my process until I finally settled on a process that I'm sharing in *CPE* and the *CPE Workbook,* which provides you with the same template worksheets that I use.

It's all about finding what works for you!

While this workbook contains the worksheets you may need or want to use in fixing your sagging middle, in developing your characters more thoroughly, in plotting out your story from start to finish, or in plotting only the few key plot points that can make a difference, this workbook does not contain all of the background information, or how to plot more effectively as is provided in the *CPE* book.

This workbook was designed as a *companion* book to the *CPE* book.

The overall design was that they would work well together.

CHAPTER 2 – WHAT THIS WORKBOOK OFFERS

This plotting workbook offers you:

- An expert—Me!
- Michael Hauge's character grid that I use as a worksheet
- My character worksheet
- My plotting worksheets using Post-it notes

While I share the detailed journey of my writing process as I encountered the Masters and fully explain the importance of integrating character, plot, and emotion—specifically how, why, and when in *CPE,* in this workbook, I detail and share just my plotting process.

This workbook is a companion to *CPE: Character, Plot, & Emotion.*

As I state in *CPE,* by no means are either of these two books the end all of plotting and of creating characters. There are many, many books on these topics, written by other writers, editors, producers, and publishers who are sharing their expertise, as well.

Why Me?

My writing process evolved over time, which included returning to school as a non-traditional student late in life, studying the pedagogy of teaching—meaning the teaching and learning of writing — where I became a university professor of writing classes.

Even though I'm no longer teaching in the classroom, my sharing and teaching continues with books, blogs, and presentations.

I enjoy helping people rediscover an earlier interest or passion for writing. So many people want to write but don't know where to start, so I've always enjoyed assisting them, helping them find a path that best fits their needs, *at that time.*

That's what this workbook can do for you. You purchased this book because you're stuck or you're experimenting, wanting to find a better way of writing.

This workbook isn't going to magically provide everything you need, but it can help you get to the next level of improvement, of being able to more easily create the story you want to finish.

You may glean a few tidbits to incorporate into your process for now, and maybe you'll come back and add a few more later. Or, maybe you'll try my entire process to see if it's a good fit for you, but then eliminate a part or two, discovering they aren't quite what you need, at this time.

This journey you're on is *your* journey. No one else's; just yours. That's your goal—to find what *you* need.

A Summary of My Plot Points Journey

To summarize my *aha moments*:

While Syd Field introduced me to the paradigm structure of a story in a screenplay format, it was Christopher Vogler who introduced me to specific and important plot points.

And then, it was Michael Hauge who layered in the importance of tying emotion to those various plot points via the character's wound with his focus on developing the main character, and how all the other three key primary characters were tied to the protagonist's wound.

I never could understand the two pinch points that Field spoke about until I realized while analyzing movies that those pinch points were often scenes from the antagonist's point of view.

What better way to show danger coming toward the protagonist than from the enemy's point of view? That move allows us to see just how powerful the antagonist is and that the protagonist could fail reaching their goal.

And then, when in 2011, I read Allen Palmer's article about the hero's emotional journey as applied to Vogler's 12 plot points (see Recommended Reading page), those one-word emotions cemented those plot points for me.

Vogler, Palmer, and Hauge

Using Vogler's plot points mixed with Hauge's terminology and percentages, along with Palmer's terminology of feeling that I added a decade later, I created:

- Storyboards, using two-fold science boards
- Post-it Plotting Worksheets (templates included in this book)
- An Outline (synopsis, treatment) Document Example

Sometimes, different stories required a different approach—storyboard or plotting worksheets—depending on how many details I know right away versus how much brainstorming I still need to do.

The storyboard allows me a huge visual for my Post-it notes that I can easily fold and slide behind a dresser or door. I don't have to take my Post-its off the wall, door, or desktop. I can easily transport the storyboard in the car when attending a write-in or when I'm meeting someone privately to brainstorm with.

The Post-it Plotting Worksheets allow me to spread the sheets on the bed, desktop, or floor and move the Post-its around easily. The sheets fit into a file folder, which allows me to travel with the file and work from any tabletop easily. Photographs of my storyboards—large science boards and a file folder storyboard—are located in the *CPE* book.

The story's length or medium doesn't matter. These plot points work for all screenplays and fiction, long or short.

*****

Choose What Works for You

I know what works for me.

I don't know what will work for you. However, having taught my methods to a vast number of writers, I've seen their *aha moments.*

In experiencing their *aha moments,* they'd uttered how their pantsering led them to a cliff, to a sagging middle, or to a point they didn't know what to do.

They said by naming and knowing just the five big plot points that Hauge repeatedly states are the key plot points that can elicit the most character emotion made their stories come alive again. Almost as if by magic. The illumination of surprise recognition on their faces looking at that storyboard was as if a room of riches had just been offered to them.

By no means have any of my teachings been adopted or adapted 100%.

This book simply represents the end results of my journey of discovery and includes what I've taught in my writing classes both inseat and online, in academic and non-academic classrooms, and what I've shared with writers in coaching sessions and presentations.

This book shares the templates and worksheets I created in my journey and includes Michael Hauge's character chart that I use in my plotting process, and which he graciously gave me permission to share with you.

His chart comes from that weekend where he first presented it in his workshop, and where I accepted that workshop as my New Opportunity as I journeyed into a new process, a new world of writing.

*****

The plot points are analyzed and discussed at length in *CPE* and include examples of how they're structural in scenes.

Here, before we get into the worksheets themselves, I've listed the Plot Points in order as they appear on the Worksheets and what goes on each Post-it note for that plot point.

CHAPTER 3 – CPE

Character, Plot, and Emotion

This chapter is about helping you develop the worksheets by my asking you questions about your characters, the plot, and the character emotions that will influence the character's decisions, thus driving the plot.

These are questions I would be asking you in a one-on-one consultation appointment.

If you're unsure of what I'm asking, I recommend you refer to the *CPE* book and read the sections of Character, Plot, and Emotion, as these questions pertain to the information contained there.

So, here we go...

Character:

- Is the main character ordinary or extraordinary?
- Are any of the other characters extraordinary?
- What is the main character's arc going to be? The lesson they need to learn? The wound they need to heal?
- What are the dangers they face: emotional, physical, psychological?
- What seemingly no-nothing skill(s) need to be shown early that they'll use in battle later?
- What skills will they learn through their Act II engagements with others or with their mentor that they'll be using against the antagonist?
- List a few of your favorite characters, and then in a word or two, state what makes each character memorable. *Why* are they a favorite? By looking more

closely at those characters, can they help you create equally likeable and memorable characters?

- What is the biggest problem the main character faces *today?*

Early in my journey, I recognized that my character's outer motivation, their visible goal was tied to Maslow's Hierarchy of Needs. *What do they need versus what do they want*? Their *want* is connected to their self-worth as they believe others see them, but their *need* is connected to their self-confidence as they see themselves.

So, the Outer Motivation concrete goal (of want) is tied to the Inner Motivation (of need) and is at war with the Inner Conflict (of the wound), per Hauge's first row on the Character Worksheet regarding the hero. The full worksheet is provided in Chapter 5:

	Outer Motivation	**Outer Conflict**	**Inner Motivation**	**Inner Conflict**
Hero				

Maslow's Hierarch of Needs

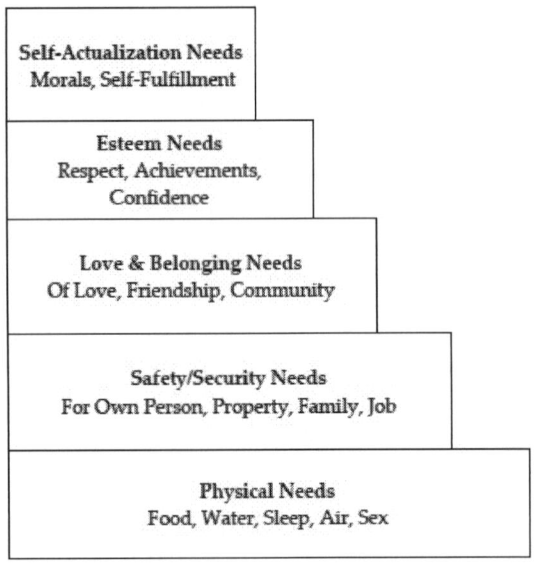

A reminder about the three other primary characters listed in Hauge's motivational and conflict character worksheet...

Nemesis: This character is embodied by the hero's Inner Conflict that has happened before the story began, or this character can embody the growth, the arc that the main character must travel. This character is generally attached to the Ghost Person or Ghost Event in some way. The nemesis also represents Outer Conflict by how they physically are blocking the hero from achieving their goal.

Reflection / Buddy: This character will help the hero achieve their goal and will reveal the hero's Inner Conflict when the hero needs to be reminded. This character isn't afraid to point out the hero's flaws or weaknesses.

Romance: This character is alternately for and against the hero, with the story having a Happily Ever After (HEA) ending once the hero's Inner Conflict is resolved.

Plot:

- Does this story require symbolism? If so, what's the object? What does the object represent? Can you use this symbol in different ways?
- Does the plot adhere to the required elements of its genre? Mystery versus science fiction, romance versus women's fiction, etc. For example:
    - In romances, there is the fear of never finding love, of losing love.
    - In quest stories, there is the fear of never finding the treasure, or the enemy finding it first and doing great harm to the treasure or using it against society.
    - In psychological thrillers, there is the fear of death.
    - In science fiction, there is the expectation of a different world with different rules.
- Does the story circle back to the ordinary world in some way?
- Is the ending satisfactory even if the protagonist dies in the end? Does their death provide a positive outcome to those who survive?

Emotion:

- How does the main character react to being in danger, whether physical, mental, emotional?

- How do they react to their mentor? How many ways can that mentor *poke the bear* (the protagonist's emotions)?
- What are the emotional relationships of other characters?
- How do those relationships change emotionally?
- What is the main character afraid of? What is that greatest fear?
- How do they react when they repeatedly face that fear?
- What is it that the protagonist is finally willing to leave behind emotionally, physically, or psychologically so that they can move forward successfully, becoming a better person?

These questions are meant to be a starting place if you're feeling stuck. If you have questions of your own, add them to the lists, or create your own list of questions to ask when starting a new story.

These are questions that can also be asked at any point in the story where you find yourself stalled in a scene.

CHAPTER 4 –THE PLOT POINTS

The Plot Points & Other Important Elements

As I progressed through my plotting journey, discovering new experts who had renamed Vogler's plot points, I found the different terminology confusing at times.

So, I created a chart (see next page) using Syd Field, Christopher Vogler, Blake Snyder, Michael Hauge, and Allen Palmer's terminology and lining up the plot points so that they made sense to me.

The last column represents the terminology I chose to use on my Post-it Plotting Worksheets, so it made sense for me, and hopefully for you, too. If not, feel free to rename a plot point so that you'll understand what it means when you see it.

1. Ordinary World
2. Throwaway line (stated) (3%)
3. New Opportunity (10%)
4. Discussion & Decision
5. Meeting Mentor
6. Change of Plans (25%)
7. Tests, Allies, & Enemies
8. Pinch Point (37%)
9. Midpoint Self Reflection (50%)
10. First Battle
11. Pinch Point (62%)
12. Celebration (False Win)
13. Major Setback where All is Lost (75%)
14. Climax
15. Claiming the Prize (99-100%)

The Comparison of Experts Chart is discussed at length in the *CPE* book.

The plot points in the chart are listed and afterward, with details of how to plot each point.

Comparison of the Experts

%	Syd Field	Chris Vogler	Blake Synder	Michael Hauge	Allen Palmer (Feelings)	CPE terminology
	Act I		Opening Image			
		Ordinary World	Setup		Incomplete	Ordinary World
3%			Theme Stated	Throwaway line		Throwaway Line
10%		Call to Adventure	Catalyst	New Opportunity	Unsettled	New Opportunity
		Refusal of the Call	Debate		Resistant	Discussion & Decision
		Meeting the Mentor	Break into 2		Encouraged	Meeting the Mentor
25%	Act II Part I	Crossing the First Threshold	B Story	Change of Plans	Committed	Change of Plans
		Tests, Allies, Enemies	Fun & Games		Disoriented	Tests, Allies, Enemies
37%	Pinch Point					Pinch Point
50%	Act II Part 2	Approach to the Innermost Cave	Midpoint	Point of No Return	Inauthentic	Midpoint Self-Reflection
		Supreme Ordeal	Bad Guys Close In		Confronted	First Battle
62%	Pinch Point					Pinch Point
		Seizing the Reward	Break Into 3		Reborn	Celebration (False Win)
75%	Act III	The Road Back	All is Lost & Dark Night of the Soul	Major Setback	Desperate	Major Setback Where All is Lost
		Resurrection	Finale 4-Part Finale	Climax	Decisive	Climax
99-100%		Return with the Elixir	Final Image		Complete	Claiming the Prize

Using Post-its

My plotting process is all about using Post-it notes. Why? Because they're easily moved, making them fluid. They come in an assortment of colors, so if I wanted, each character could be a different color. Or, I could use one color for the main character's actions and decisions, another color for emotional responses, and so forth.

Post-it notes are an easy way to begin a story. You'll see how specifically later.

Should you come to a Post-it where you don't know what to write, don't panic. Skip it. You can come back to it later. You'll see in my story example later in Chapter 6, where I had empty spaces in my initial plotting session.

So, for each of these Post-its, record what you know. Leave blank what you don't know for now.

All you need are just a few words for each Post-it or a short phrase.

Before the Journey Begins

Post-its 1-6

1. Title / Genre / Setting / Timeline: just record each of these story elements.

2. Key Question: Write the question that can be asked throughout the entire story and answered by the story's end. Ideally, the Key Question is tied to every scene either through character or by plot events.

3. Overall Theme: Record what you believe is the overall theme.

4. Ghost Event or Ghost Person: Name the person or event.

   As a side note: When a mentor read my first novel, a romance, she told me that I needed to cut off the first three chapters—the equivalent of 60 pages—telling me it was *backstory*. I was shocked at how many pages needed to be cut, but she was right.

   Don't be surprised if you suddenly find yourself writing a page or multiple pages of information with enthusiasm as you think about your story. Why? Because the backstory is a *trigger*. You're thinking about your character and their history starts flowing. You want to record it so you can use bits and pieces throughout the story as the character reconciles with their past, but this information shouldn't start the story.

Just as this backstory is triggering you, consider how this ghost event or ghost person has been triggering the main character their entire life as a ghost and something the character doesn't want revealed, at least not right away.

This is a great time to write each trigger on a separate Post-it note. You'll see why later. In fact, any relevant piece of information you imagine being told at some point in the story, write it down as a separate Post-it note. Then, just stack them under the named person or event.

5. Prologue: All you need here is a word or short phrase to summarize what this prologue scene will entail; such as: spouse murdered, abused as a child, first kiss, high school prom, and so forth. Are you already hearing the dialogue, seeing the action? Write it up! Set it aside. More on what to do with these early writings later.

   If you don't have a prologue, that's fine. Leave the square blank.

6. Opening Image: Use just a few words to describe what the opening image looks like.

Primary Plot Points
Post-its 7-30

Post-its 7-12

7. Ordinary World: Write a few words of what this Ordinary World looks like.
8. Theme Stated: Write the throwaway line, what you hear the buddy / mentor saying after they've questioned the main character with *Do you know what your problem is?*
9. New Opportunity (10%): What New Opportunity has been presented to the main character?
10. Discussion & Decision: Who does the main character talk with initially about this major opportunity that is offered and what is their initial thought?
11. Meeting the Mentor: While at first the protagonist wants the mentor to agree with their decision, at the same time, the protagonist is asking, *Was I wrong not to say yes*

to the New Opportunity? In a few words, how does this meeting go?

12. Change of Plans (25%): There is a physical or mental crossover into a new world, a new way of thinking. Everything feels alien, not at all normal. In a phrase or few words, what's new about this world?

Post-its 13-18

13. Tests, Allies, Enemies: The protagonist meets new people, is put in new situations, and is being tested. Name these tests and people.

14. Pinch Point (37%): This plot point is where we get our first glimpse of the real enemy the protagonist is battling. Describe in a few words, how we see this enemy at this point in the story.

15. Mid-Point Self-Reflection (50%): As a mirror moment, how does the protagonist see themself for the first time in truth, and as others have seen them all along?

16. First Battle: A crisis has occurred, and they've survived. The protagonist has faced their enemy or fear and won. They overcame the confrontation. With a few words describe that confrontation.

17. Pinch Point (62%): This plot point is our second glimpse of the dark force approaching the protagonist. This pinch point will appear more threatening than the first pinch point did. What is this pinch point?

18. Celebration (False Win): Even though the protagonist has won this First Battle, they continue to struggle with whom they want to become, wanting to dismantle their wound totally. Deep in their heart, they sense the war isn't over, and they worry they won't be good enough. With a few words, what occurs at this plot point?

Post-its 19-24

19. Major Setback Where All is Lost (75%): This plot point is significant. Everything gained so far is gone. Describe the protagonist's fear, the quandary they're now in.

20. Climax (90-99%): This plot point is the start of the 4-Part Finale, where each part has its own Post-it note. The complexity and genre of your story will determine if you use all 4 parts or not. Provide a word that best describes the Climax.

21. Finale Plan: In a few words, describe the plan. Is the protagonist acting alone or is there a group creating the plan?

22. Finale Storm: Describe the action performed to implement the plan.

23. Finale Trapped: In a few words, describe the trap.

24. Finale Final Battle: How does the protagonist's old self die? What *do or die* action do they take?

Post-its 25-30

25. Claiming the Prize: In a few words, describe the reveal, how the story ends.

26. Final Image: What is the last image you want to give your audience?

27. Protagonist: This space is where you can create a Post-it from the Character Square Worksheet and one for each of the following characters, or you may decide you want to record attributes—physical or otherwise—here as you develop the worksheets. You choose how you use these last four squares.

28. Antagonist: Same as protagonist.

29. Buddy / Mentor / Reflection: Same as protagonist.

30. Love Interest (Fake Antagonist): Same as protagonist.

CHAPTER 5 – THE WORKSHEETS

The purpose of creating *CPE Workbook* as an 8.5 x 11" book was so that I could replicate the Worksheets in true size.

The purpose of creating two copies of each template set is so you can tear one set out of this Workbook for copying or scanning, while keeping the second set safe, inside the book.

Tools Required for Post-it Notes Plotting

The sheets are designed so that a Post-it note fits inside each square. If needed, Post-it notes can be stacked within a square. You'll need:

- standard 3x3 inch Post-it notes
- a printed version of the worksheets

A Suggestion

As you work with any of these worksheets, I know from plotting my own stories and from working with other writers, the ideas will start flowing fast and furious. Be prepared!

Your goal is to capture those ideas quickly in writing, so that you don't lose them.

How you record them will be up to you. Me? If just an idea, I'll use a Post-it note, but if I start hearing a conversation or am visualizing the scene unfolding, I'll quickly record the scene *without editing* either by keyboard or by paper and pencil. More on how to manage these mini recordings later in Chapter 6.

Feel free to work back and forth among these worksheets, as well. You're under no obligation to first fill out one before moving on to the next. Use whatever method or order that *works for you*!

Character Worksheets

Michael Hauge's Worksheet

This character worksheet, a grid that establishes character motivation and conflict comes from Michael Hauge's book, *Writing Screenplays That Sell* and is being used with his permission.

Be sure to fill in the hero's line completely. How you fill in the other lines will depend on your story and its genre, which is explained more fully in *CPE.*

While this first worksheet replicates Hauge's terminology, I've used other names for these characters throughout the *CPE* book and in this workbook. For your benefit, I'm listing the various names used in both books here.

Each character can be of any sex, any age. In fact, any of them could be characters of fantasy, such as a dragon, fairies, an ogre, a shapeshifter, and so forth.

- Hero, also known as the protagonist or main character.
- Nemesis, also known as the antagonist or enemy.
- Reflection character, also known as the Buddy or Mentor.
- Romance character, also known as the Fake Antagonist.

Sometimes, the nemesis can be the weather, the environment, or even an animal. Stories that come to mind are *The Old Man and the Sea, Jaws,* and *The Grey.*

Examples where the protagonist isn't human are *Shrek, Watership Down, The Call of the Wild,* and *Charlotte's Web.*

Regardless of who the protagonist is and who the other characters are, the plot point structure applies to all stories.

- Outer Motivation is the physical / concrete goal / *want*.
- Outer Conflict is what's blocking the protagonist's Outer Motivation.
- Inner Motivation is what they really *need.*
- Inner Conflict is the wound that creates the need, from which they created their lie.

From Michael Hauge's book, *Writing Screenplays That Sell,* used with permission.

	Outer Motivation	Outer Conflict	Inner Motivation	Inner Conflict
Hero				
Nemesis				
Reflection				
Romance				

From Michael Hauge's book, *Writing Screenplays That Sell,* used with permission.

	Outer Motivation	Outer Conflict	Inner Motivation	Inner Conflict
Hero				
Nemesis				
Reflection				
Romance				

Dr. Diana's Worksheet

I developed this 1999 worksheet of *Putting a Square Peg into a Round Hole* as I read and listened to various writers:

I learned story characters are dealing with insecurities, faults, wounds, flaws, feeling insecure and awkward, because they didn't fit into their Ordinary World.

These elements of characteristic traits, including a wound, and a lie, in addition to flaws give characters depth. Depth that had been lacking in my characters.

I saw them as a square peg trying to fit into an otherwise round world, hence the creation of my character square and creating four unique character traits with the wound at their core, which then can influence each of those traits.

To assist in the brainstorming of those traits, I installed the business model of the SWOT diagram, as a reminder to identify the character's Strengths, Weaknesses, Opportunities, and Threats.

And then finally, at the bottom of my worksheet, I listed Wound, Fear, Life, Secret, and Wound Triggers to help me specifically identify each of these elements that are solidly connected to the character's wound.

The wound features their fear, which they've kept secret all this time, but will be revealed later in the story.

The Wound Triggers, which I name at least three, are reminders for me to include in the plotting of the story, where the main character will butt up again them as they journey through their arc.

Putting a Square Peg into a Round World

Dr. Diana's Creating Characters Worksheet

Name:	Name:

Use SWOT techniques – Strengths, Weaknesses, Opportunities, and Threats

Strengths	Weaknesses
Opportunities	**Threats**

Strengths	Weaknesses
Opportunities	**Threats**

Wound:

Fear:

Lie:

Secret:

Wound Triggers:

Putting a Square Peg into a Round World
Dr. Diana's Creating Characters Worksheet

Name:	Name:

Use SWOT techniques – Strengths, Weaknesses, Opportunities, and Threats

Strengths	Weaknesses
Opportunities	**Threats**

Strengths	Weaknesses
Opportunities	**Threats**

Wound:

Fear:

Lie:

Secret:

Wound Triggers:

Post-it Plotting Worksheets

The Post-it Plotting Worksheets (2 copies of each set) include the following:

- A worksheet with only lines, divided so that a Post-it will fit in each square. This page is one you can use to:
  - Create a character brainstorming worksheet of your own design.
  - Create just the 5 major plot points that Michael Hauge states are prime story areas to "elicit maximum emotion."
  - Create worksheets where you rename the labels, using labels that better help you identify the plot points.
  - Create worksheets where you create specific instructions for each square.
- The primary set of worksheets are five pre-labeled pages with the *CPE* plot points, as depicted in the last column of the Comparison of the Experts chart in Chapter 3.

Chapter 6 yields yet another set of the CPE Post-it Plotting Worksheets, demonstrating how I first drafted a story recently published earlier this year.

When creating your Post-it notes, you'll want to use phrases, strong active words. Less is more, because you'll be using these Post-it notes to *read* your story across the sheets or on the storyboard.

You don't want to get stalled or bogged down with story details at this point. You want that reading to move quickly but smoothly.

1 - Title / Genre / Setting	2 – Key Question
3 – Overall Theme	**4 – Ghost Event or Person**
5 - Prologue	**6 – Opening Image**

7 – Ordinary World

8 – Theme Stated (3)

9 - New Opportunity (10%)

10 – Discussion & Decision (Debate)

11 – Meeting the Mentor

12 – Change of Plans (25%)

13 - Test, Allies, Enemies	14 - Pinch Point (37%)
15 - Mid-Point Self-Reflection (50%)	16 – First Battle
17 – Pinch Point (62%)	18 – Celebration (False Win)

19 - Major Setback (75%)	20 – Climax / Finale (90-99%)
21 – Finale Plan	**22 – Finale Storm**
23 – Finale Trapped	**24 – Finale Final Battle**

25 – Claiming the Prize

26 – Final Image

27 - Protagonist

28 - Antagonist

29- Buddy / Mentor / Reflection

30 – Love Interest (Fake Antagonist)

1 - Title / Genre / Setting	2 – Key Question
3 – Overall Theme	**4 – Ghost Event or Ghost Person**
5 - Prologue	**6 – Opening Image**

7 – Ordinary World

8 – Theme Stated (3)

9 - New Opportunity (10%)

10 – Discussion & Decision (Debate)

11 – Meeting the Mentor

12 – Change of Plans (25%)

13 - Test, Allies, Enemies

14 - Pinch Point (37%)

15 - Mid-Point Self-Reflection (50%)

16 – First Battle

17 – Pinch Point (62%)

18 – Celebration (False Win)

19 - Major Setback (75%)

20 – Climax / Finale (90-99%)

21 – Finale Plan

22 – Finale Storm

23 – Finale Trapped

24 – Finale Final Battle

25 – Claiming the Prize

26 – Final Image

27 - Protagonist

28 - Antagonist

29- Buddy / Mentor / Reflection

30 – Love Interest (Fake Antagonist)

Chapter 6 - Dr. Diana's Plotting Process

Steps 1-7

As I created and collected helpful cheat sheets and notes that serve as reminders when plotting, I placed them in a binder. This binder has become my plotting go-to at the start of every story.

The binder contains sets of my worksheets, list of questions, how-to articles I've saved, and anything that will help remind me to include as I plot through my characters, the plot, and their emotions.

Step 1

My first step is to write what I call *character journals.* Their journal is always written in first person. This method allows me to get into their head, and soon, I can hear their voice. Their sentences are flavored with that voice, their way of talking, observing, and thinking.

Basically, it's a long diary entry that the character dictates, and it's as if they've never done one before. Naturally, they start at the beginning, providing basic physical descriptions of themselves: height, weight, color of hair, eyes, scars from injuries, etc. Then, they start telling me about their parents, their problems, what it was like in school, jobs they've had, dreams and desires.

Anytime they gloss over a problem or something in the past, I'll ask questions, like:

How did that feel?

What did you do then?

In asking questions, I'm digging down with a goal to uncover their wound. Eventually, I can hear a change in their voice, and that's where I really drill down, asking questions. Sure enough, the wound is there and is revealed but with a promise I won't tell anyone else. I always promise.

I know that they'll reveal their wound by the end of the written story, but for now it's our secret.

It may take me several days to write journals for the primary characters. From their wounds, I'm able to create plot point events that have them butting up against their wound—repeatedly.

Step #2

Now, I'm able to fill in the two character worksheets—Hauge's and mine—making sure the wound is solid enough to engage the other primary characters and who will propel the main character to *want* to change, to become a better person, or achieve their goal or quest. My plotting goal is that by the story's end, the character has become so well-rounded that they no longer can fit into that square box where they'd been caged in the earlier Ordinary World.

Let me give you an example of how these characteristics can help you create plot.

Let's say my character is a nurse. The four traits are *caring, determined, detailed*, and *keeps to herself*. Her wound is that her father died when he became ill and was hospitalized. It's a reason why she became a nurse.

This outcome is a boring character. The dialogue will be shallow. We've created a caricature of a nurse.

Let's change one of the four traits. Instead of *caring*, let's make her *revengeful.*

Combined with *determined, detailed, keeps to herself,* and the reason why she became a nurse—getting revenge—can you see the possibilities of better scenes, story, and ending? Dialogue will now be filled with subtext. Words coming from a caring nurse will mean something entirely different coming from a revengeful nurse.

Step #3

By rereading the character journals and re-examining the two character worksheets, I create Post-it notes for action scenes, of triggers, feelings, conversations, clues, anything that could be used in a scene. There's no judging, no deleting, just a collection of potential scenes. I don't worry whether I have too many or don't feel I have enough.

I don't worry about scene point of view, either. That determination will develop further along my steps.

Step #4

Using my plotting worksheets, I spread them out so I can see them all in one glance.

I start sorting through the Post-it notes, grouping them as needed. I may place them above or below an appropriate sheet, but I don't place them on any sheet yet.

Right now, I'm searching for those five big key plot points of New Opportunity, Change of Plans, Midpoint Self-Reflection, Major Setback Where All is Lost, and the Climax. The scenes that will create maximum emotion; meaning, they'll make the audience cry, laugh, fall in love with the character, and so forth; *and,* where the story can and should spin in a different direction, all because of what has happened to the main character based on an earlier decision.

If any of those five scenes aren't in the pile, then I have to brainstorm what they would be. I go back to the journal and character worksheets and do some more brainstorming. I consult my brainstorming binder that contains tips, tricks, and everything I want to remember to do when plotting. Also, I consult my various thesaurus books on emotion, emotional wounds, emotion amplifiers, conflict, and negative traits—a series of books published by Angela Ackerman and Becca Puglisi.

These five scenes are the scenes that need to be placed on the plotting sheets first.

Why?

Because the story is built around and between them.

The main character's emotions, based on their wound or trying to overcome it, drive their decision at each of these points, flipping the story around, moving the story forward and moving the character through their arc, until they arrive at the Claiming the Prize plot point where they have finally emerged into their new self, having fought the last battle during the Climax.

Once again, those five key plot points are:

- New Opportunity (10%)
- Change of Plans (25%)
- Midpoint, Self-Reflection (50%)

- Major Setback Where All is Lost (75%)
- Climax (90-99%)

The goal in using just these five plot points is to ratchet up the tension, much like going uphill on a roller coaster, especially as we move through Act II, particularly from the Midpoint on until we reach the Climax / Finale.

It's only at the Climax / Finale that we crest the top of the roller coaster and start screaming toward the end of the ride, the end of the story. Done properly, this last twenty-five percent of the book becomes a true page-turner or has the audience on the edge of their seats.

When helping writers who are struggling with a sagging middle, I ask them to pull out these same five key plot points and place them on the sheets.

Once this bare-bone plot is exposed, the writers can easily see where emotion was lacking or how plot points were positioned wrong because the tension wasn't rising. Most of the time, their Major Setback was placed as a Midpoint. Just that slight correction made an enormous difference!

Step #5

Once the five key plot points are in position, now it becomes relatively easy to fill in the remaining plot points, bridging between and among the first five already established.

This is where I'm putting the Post-it notes into position, much like putting pieces of a jigsaw puzzle together.

This is where using Post-it notes are advantageous because they're easy to move around, whether I'm using the plotting worksheets or have moved to the bigger science board because the story is more complex or has more than one timeline.

The beauty of Post-it notes on a storyboard is that the storyboard can be folded up, without having to pick up or remove the Post-it notes. Everything stays intact until your next session.

Step #6

Once I've *read* my Post-it notes from start to finish, with the character's growth and the rising tension of the plot positioned properly, I move to the computer and start transferring the Post-it notes material into my Outline Document, which I provide as an example at the end of this chapter.

I call this my magic document because it contains everything regarding my story. In the beginning, the document is a template that I'm filling in. I'm listing:

- My plot points as shown on the plotting sheets.
- Any written, detailed paragraphs of dialogue or action, which get placed under the appropriate plot point.
- Anything I need to remember about my characters (under their own sections).
- Notes of anything I need to research.
- Reminders of things I need to include.
- Any brainstorming lists. (I don't delete these lists until the first draft is finished and am certain I no longer need the list.)

I record these details, knowing they could be moved within the document before finding their final home.

This document goes through many transformations before it becomes my final outline / synopsis / treatment from which I then write the first draft of my story.

I don't start writing my story until I'm no longer tinkering with the outline. At this point, the outline is done.

Although, it can be said that an outline is never really done until the story is done. Why? Because that's where the pantsering catches me off guard. A surprise occurs; a surprise I never saw coming until I was writing the first draft.

My outlines can be anywhere from 10 to 60 pages long, depending on how many scenes I wrote hurriedly while creating the Post-it notes during the brainstorming stage. Scenes that I could hear or see and didn't want to lose or forget.

An Important Hint

All of my documents received a title, which is followed by today's date. Example: CPE Workbook 3-19-24. I change the title as the document evolves from an outline to a manuscript draft. Example: CPE outline 3-24-24, CPE draft 4-1-24.

Any time I open the latest draft document, I immediately do a *Save As* and redo the date—always using today's date. By saving the document every day I touch it and rename it, I'm prevented from losing the document altogether or discovering it has been corrupted. I can always retract text from an earlier version should I need it.

Once the book is published, I go back and deleted most of those drafts, keeping the first one, the last one, and a few here and there in the middle.

My Outline Document is always my starting place. It keeps me organize, allows me to unload everything in my head onto paper.

The secret of brainstorming is to create a flow, and that can only occur once you get all your thoughts on paper. By keeping everything in your head, you forget, and you're creating a dam of sorts.

As to the Post-it notes...once I'm done with them, I stick the pile into my archive notebook, where a copy of my printed outline will go, and eventually my final draft.

Step #7

Now that I can't add anything more to my Outline Document, I start writing the first draft of the story on the computer, thus the lack of spacing on the template is never an issue.

So, do I write my story linearly? Not always. I go where that day's passion leads me if I'm hearing dialogue or seeing a scene acted out on the movie screen of my mind.

My goal is to write this first draft *fast!*

As the story grows, the outline disappears, and the story turns into a true manuscript with chapters instead of plot point tag lines that were listed on the Outline Document, which I share with you now. Should you want an outline template, create one that works for you!

I hope this *CPE Workbook* has helped you get unstuck. May writing your drafts fill you with joy once again.

Happy Writing!

Outline Document

(% plot points – maximum emotion plot points)

Title

Key Question – Why Now?

Setting & Timeline

Theme

Symbolism?

Ghost Event / Person

Characters

Protagonist –

Antagonist / Nemesis –

Mentor / Buddy –

Romance / False Villain –

Other Characters:

Name –

Name –

Name –

List any incidences that implement the Magic of 3

ACT I

PROLOGUE

OPENING IMAGE

SETUP / ORDINARY WORLD – How are they *feeling incomplete?*

THEME STATED AS THROWAWAY LINE by Buddy or Mentor: *You know what your problem is?*

10% NEW OPPORTUNITY, Call to Adventure, Catalyst – *feeling unsettled.*
(Romance: Main characters meet; Mystery: crime discovered, etc.)

DISCUSSION & DECISION, Refusal of the Call, Debate (with everyone but mentor) – *feeling resistant.*

MEETING THE MENTOR, Break into Act II, more discussion – *feeling encouraged.*

ACT II- Part I

(Progress: the plan appears to be working, everything appears to be going well)

25% CHANGE OF PLANS, New Beginnings, Crossing the Threshold, B Story introduced – *feeling committed.*

TESTS, ALLIES, & ENEMIES, Fun & Games – *feeling disorientated.*

37% Pinch Point – glimpse of dark force lurking from enemy POV

ACT II – Part 2

(Progress: everything becomes more complicated, stakes rise)

50% MIDPOINT SELF-RELFECTION, Approach to Innermost Cave, Point of No Return, Bridges Burned, False High, Mirror Moment, death of original external goal, set new goal – *feeling inauthentic.*

FIRST BATTLE, Supreme Ordeal, Bad Guys Close In, Crises (feeling doubt, pride, jealously, immense desire to win, world disintegrating, feeling slapped in the face, facing flaw, say aloud/think of what they fear while protecting heart, body, mind) - *feeling confronted.*

62% Pinch Point – Glimpse of dark force from enemy POV, adds to final push.

CELEBRATION (FALSE WIN), Seizing the reward, character demonstrates they have changed – *feeling reborn.*

ACT III - Resolve

75% MAJOR SETBACK WHERE ALL IS LOST, The Road Back, Dark Night of the Soul, complications, wants to retreat but can't, needs to choose between what they want and what they need, which is doing the right thing – *feeling desperate.*

CLIMAX, final with 4-part finale, Resurrection, Rebirth, Do or Die – *feeling decisive.*

1. Team gathers, makes a plan.
2. Execute the plan, storm ahead.
3. Trapped!
4. Do or Die.

CLAIMING THE PRIZE, Return Home with the Elixir – *feeling complete.*

FINAL IMAGE

RECOMMENDED READING

BOOKS

The Anatomy of Genres, John Truby
The Anatomy of Story: 22 Steps to Becoming a Master Storyteller, John Truby
Creating Unforgettable Characters, Linda Seger
The Hero's 2 Journey, Michael Hauge & Christopher Vogler (DVD)
How to Write a Novel Using the Snowflake Method, Randy Ingermanson
Poetics, Aristotle
The Power of Myth, Joseph Campbell
Save the Cat! (on screenwriting), Sydney Blake
Save the Cat! Writes a Novel, Jessica Brody
Screenplay, Syd Field
Storytelling Made Easy, Michael Hauge
Techniques of the Selling Writer, Dwight V. Swain
Write Your Novel From the Middle, James Scott Bell
The Writer's Journey, Christopher Vogler
Writing Screenplays that Sell, Michael Hauge
Writing for Story, Jon Franklin
Your Storytelling Potential, Mitchell German

ARTICLES

"A New Character-Driven Hero's Journey," *Cracking Yarns.* Allen Palmer, April 4, 2021. http://www.crackingyarns.com.au/2011/04/04/a-new-character-driven-heros-journey-2/

"The Five-Step Finale," *Save the Cat!* Blake Snyder. December 17, 2007. https://savethecat.com/tips-and-tactics/the-five-step-finale

About the Author

Diana Stout, MFA, Ph.D. is an award-winning writer, who taught writing classes for a decade online, then returned to school as a nontraditional student, so she could combine her two passions of teaching and writing and become an accredited English professor, teaching writing classes in college classrooms. Her students told her, "You smile when you talk about writing."

"A writer to watch." She's a screenwriter, author, editor, and writing coach. She's been published across the genres, in multiple media, both traditionally and as an indie publisher through her company, Sharpened Pencils Productions LLC.

Today, she writes full time. Her greatest joy after publishing her books of fiction, nonfiction, and screenplays is helping other writers. She achieves this through her how-to books, teaching classes, and as a speaker to writing groups.

When not writing, she enjoys movies, reading, and jigsaw puzzles.

Follow Diana Stout

You can follow links to her social media from her website, Sharpened Pencils Productions: https://sharpenedpencilsproductions.com

Blogs

Behind the Scenes – life as a writer: dianastout.net
Into the Core – paranormal experiences: dianastout.com
Featured Guests with Diana Stout: dianastout.org

Also by Diana Stout

Epic Fantasy
Grendel's Mother

Romance
Determined Hearts
Love's New Beginnings
Tomorrow's Wish for Love

Laurel Ridge Novella Series
Shattered Dreams #1
Burning Desire #2
Arrested Pleasures #3
Buried Hearts #4
Tangled Passions #5
Reserved Yearnings #6
Sweet Cravings #7

Literary / Short Story
Maggie's Story

Anthology / Collections
Lost and Found (contributor & editor, anthology)

Screenplays published as books
David & Goliath
Charlie's Christmas Carole

Nonfiction
The Super Simple Easy Basic Cookbook
Finding Your Fire & Keeping It Hot

Can You Help?

I hope you have found this plotting workbook helpful. Please consider leaving a review.

Reviews can be short, such as:

- I loved this book!
- I liked this book and found it helpful.
- This book has made me a better writer by making me a better plotter.

It's not the length of a review that counts; it's the number of reviews that a book receives.

THANK YOU!

You can leave the same review at multiple locations. These are three such locations. While each link leads to my profile page, you can click on the actual book you want to review.

BookBub | Goodreads
Amazon

I appreciate your support!

Made in the USA
Columbia, SC
04 May 2024

35238307R00046